Latino American Civil Rights

Hispanic Americans: Major Minority

Latino American Civil Rights

Thomas Arkham

Mason Crest

Mason Crest
370 Reed Road
Broomall, Pennsylvania 19008
www.masoncrest.com

Printed and bound in the United States of America.

First printing
9 8 7 6 5 4 3 2 1

Library of Congress Cataloging-in-Publication Data

Arkham, Thomas.
  Latino American civil rights / by Thomas Arkham.
    p. cm. — (Hispanic Americans : major minority)
  Includes index.
  ISBN 978-1-4222-2319-2 (hardcover) — ISBN 978-1-4222-2315-4 (hardcover series) — ISBN
978-1-4222-9323-2 (ebook)
  1. Hispanic Americans—Civil rights—Juvenile literature. I. Title.
  E184.S75A86 2012
  323.1168′073—dc22
                        2010052516

Produced by Harding House Publishing Services, Inc.
www.hardinghousepages.com
Interior design by Micaela Sanna.
Cover design by Torque Advertising + Design.
Printed in USA.

Contents

Introduction

by José E. Limón, Ph.D.

Even before there was a United States, Hispanics were present in what would become this country. Beginning in the sixteenth century, Spanish explorers traversed North America, and their explorations encouraged settlement as early as the sixteenth century in what is now northern New Mexico and Florida, and as late as the mid-eighteenth century in what is now southern Texas and California.

Later, in the nineteenth century, following Spain's gradual withdrawal from the New World, Mexico in particular established its own distinctive presence in what is now the southwestern part of the United States, a presence reinforced in the first half of the twentieth century by substantial immigration from that country. At the close of the nineteenth century, the U.S. war with Spain brought Cuba and Puerto Rico into an interactive relationship with the United States, the latter in a special political and economic affiliation with the United States even as American power influenced the course of almost every other Latin American country.

The books in this series remind us of these historical origins, even as each explores the present reality of different Hispanic groups. Some of these books explore the contemporary social origins—what social scientists call the "push" factors—behind the accelerating Hispanic immigration to America: political instability, economic underdevelopment and crisis, environmental degradation, impoverished or wholly absent educational systems, and other circumstances contribute to many Latin Americans deciding they will be better off in the United States.

And, for the most part, they will be. The vast majority come to work and work very hard, in order to earn better wages than they would back home. They fill significant labor needs in the U.S. economy and contribute to the economy through lower consumer prices and sales taxes.

When they leave their home countries, many immigrants may initially fear that they are leaving behind vital and important aspects of their home cultures: the Spanish language, kinship ties, food, music, folklore, and the arts. But as these books also make clear, culture is a fluid thing, and these native cultures are not only brought to America, they are also replenished in the United States in fascinating and novel ways. These books further suggest to us that Hispanic groups enhance American culture as a whole.

Our country—especially the young, future leaders who will read these books—can only benefit by the fair and full knowledge these authors provide about the socio-historical origins and contemporary cultural manifestations of America's Hispanic heritage.

Details of this mural in Santa Fe, New Mexico, are shown at the beginning of each chapter in the book. The mural depicts the struggle for Latino Civil Rights in the United States.

chapter 1
What Are Civil Rights, Anyway?

Civil rights is a term you might have heard before. Maybe you took part in your school's Martin Luther King, Jr. Day. Maybe you've heard about civil rights in social studies class. But even if you think you know what civil rights are, it's still a confusing idea.

Civil Rights and the Early United States

Civil rights have always been important to America. People first came to America because they didn't like the way the king in England was treating them. Many people came to America to worship God the way they wanted, or to make some money. As time passed, more and more people came to America.

At first, the **colonies** in North America were still part of England. But the people living there weren't happy. England could tax them without asking them. The people were tired of not having rights under British rule. They fought for change. They won the Revolutionary War. The United States was born.

The men who led the new country wrote a set of rules. This is called the Constitution. The part of the Constitution that talks about rights is called the Bill of Rights. It gave Americans the freedoms and rights we still have today.

Colonies *are places where people from another country have come to live and build a new home.*

Marching for Civil Rights.

The Bill of Rights gives people what are called civil rights. They are the basic rights all humans should have. The Bill of Rights says that Americans have the freedom to print opinions in newspapers and books. Americans can say what they want. Americans can worship God how-

Hispanics are the fastest growing minority in the United States. They are also the biggest minority group. As of 2009, there are almost 50 million Hispanic people in the United States!

ever they want. They have the right to carry weapons to defend themselves. Because of the Bill of Rights, people who are accused of a crime have to have a fair trial with a lawyer. And all Americans are protected from being tortured.

The Bill of Rights has been around for more than two hundred years. But the United States hasn't always protected the rights of everyone. African Americans didn't get the same rights as everyone else. At first, Black Americans were not considered citizens. Most of them had come to the United States as slaves. The Constitution even said that slaves only counted as three-fifths of a person!

Civil Rights for Everyone

During the middle of the 1800s, the United States split into two parts. The North and South fought each other. This was called the Civil War. Slavery was the big problem. The North won the war. After the war, the slaves were freed. But they still didn't have civil rights.

Black Americans were often badly treated. This led to the civil rights movement. The civil rights movement started in the 1950s. People like Dr. Martin Luther King, Jr., Malcolm X, Rosa Parks, and others fought for African Americans' right. Today, a lot has changed. African Americans still aren't always treated the same as white Americans, though.

To discriminate means to treat a group of people differently than everybody else, usually worse.

Black Americans aren't the only ones who have been treated badly in America. Hispanic Americans have also had problems in the United States. People often **discriminate** against them. Sometimes, Hispanics get paid less than white Americans for doing the same job. Sometimes, people don't even want Hispanics to live in their neighborhoods. Hispanics face a situation that is just as tough as many black people face.

chapter 2
Fighting for Justice: Hispanic Americans Over the Years

Have you ever looked at your family tree? Do you know if your grandmother or great-grandfather came to the United States from a different country? Whether you know it or not, someone in your family was probably an immigrant. Maybe your **ancestors** came from England hundreds of years ago. Maybe your parents were born in India.

Almost all Americans are the children, grandchildren, great-grandchildren (or many greats!) of immigrants. The only people who aren't **descendants** of immigrants are people whose ancestors were the **Native** people who lived in America before the people from Europe arrived. Somebody in your family came to America by boat, wagon, car, or plane from someplace else!

Hispanic Americans are one group of immigrants to the United States. But some of them have lived here longer than anyone else except the Native people!

Ancestors *are the people in a family who were born in the past, sometimes a very long time ago.*

Descendants *are the people in a family related to the same ancestor.*

Native *means the people who have lived in a place for a long time. It can also mean the culture of those people.*

Where Did Hispanic Americans Come From?

> **Culture** *is a word people use to talk about a group of people. These people probably come from the same place. They probably speak the same language. They may believe the same things about God. They share lots of beliefs. They do many things the same way.*

Let's look back at history. Hundreds of years ago, the Spanish took over most of what we call Latin America. They killed many of the Native people who lived there. The Spanish brought with them their germs. Some of the Natives got sick and died from these new germs. But not all the Natives died.

Some of the Native people married Spanish people. Children were born who had one Spanish parent and one Native parent. They were a mix of both Spanish and Native. Today's Hispanics came from these children. Hispanic **culture** is a mix of these two peoples. Hispanic food is a mixture of the two cultures. So is Hispanic art and music.

The first encounter between Spain and North America.

WHAT IS LATIN AMERICA?

The Spanish-speaking countries in North and South America are called Latin America. They include:

- Mexico
- Guatemala
- El Salvador
- Honduras
- Nicaragua
- Costa Rica
- Panama

- Cuba
- Dominican Republic
- Venezuela
- Colombia
- Ecuador
- Peru
- Bolivia

- Paraguay
- Uruguay
- Argentina
- Chile
- Puerto Rico (part of the United States)
- Brazil

Hispanics in the United States

Lots of Hispanic Americans didn't actually come to the United States. Instead, the United States came to them! Until the middle of the 1800s, what is now the southwestern United States belonged to Mexico. This included most of Texas, California, New Mexico, Arizona, Colorado, Nevada, and Utah. In 1848, Mexico and the United States came to an agreement. They agreed that this land would now be part of the United States.

Their agreement let people in this area become U.S. citizens if they wanted. If a Mexican family was living in southern Texas, they suddenly became American. However, most people spoke Spanish. They didn't always understand the culture of their new country.

People often took advantage of the new Americans. They tricked them into leaving their land. Or they scared them off.

You've probably learned about how bad things were for African Americans after the Civil War. This was a very bad time for black people in America. But you may not know that Hispanic Americans had it just as bad. Some people believe that history books often ignore the problems of the Hispanic people. White people killed more Mexicans in the Southwest between 1865 and 1920 than they did black Americans in the Southeast during the same years.

HISPANIC OR LATINO?

In the 1980s, the U.S. government came up with the name "Hispanic" for people who speak Spanish and live in the United States. Not everyone likes this name. Many people don't like the way the term lumps everyone together based only on language. The people in North and South America who speak Spanish have a very different culture from Spain's. Other people use the word "Latino" for this same group of people. They like this word better because it has more to do with Latin America than with Spain.

The fact that Hispanics—or Latinos—don't agree on which term to use for themselves shows how diverse they are. They come from many different countries. They have different stories. But at the same time, Hispanic American cultures have many things in common. They share many of the same stories. They often worship God the same way. Many of the same things are important to them. They are proud of their art and music. They celebrate the same holidays.

The Beginning of Hispanic Immigration

Up until the 1920s, the Hispanics who lived in the United States had mostly been born here. They weren't immigrants. Then American factories and farms grew bigger. They needed more workers. There weren't enough Americans who wanted to take the new jobs. Factory and farm owners went to other countries to look for workers. Some went to Mexico and Central America. They convinced millions of people to come to the United States to work. Almost two million people came just from Mexico.

Many people in Mexico at that time were very poor. People didn't have jobs. People wanted jobs, even if it meant traveling all the way to the United States. Many Mexicans entered the United States to work for a short time. This situation seemed to help everyone. The United States factories and farms gained workers. Mexican workers earned money to make a living.

Many Latinos moved to America to work on farms.

Latino children will be some of tomorrow's leaders.

But not everything worked out well for the workers. The immigrants weren't treated the same as white Americans. They got less money for their work. They had trouble finding places to live. Other Americans often thought of the Mexicans as invaders. They thought the immigrants took work away from Americans. They didn't realize that most Americans didn't actually want those factory and farm jobs.

After the 1920s, the United States wanted the immigrants to go back to Mexico. The United States and Mexico came up with a plan to send

LATINO AMERICAN CIVIL RIGHTS

Mexican immigrants back to Mexico. Nobody asked the immigrants where they wanted to live. Instead, almost half a million of them were **deported** to Mexico.

Sometimes families were broken up. If you were born in the United States, you are a U.S. citizen. It doesn't matter where your parents were born. Some Mexicans had children while working here, so those children were U.S. citizens. Their parents were still Mexican. These children were often left behind while Mexican parents were sent back to Mexico.

> *If someone is* **deported,** *she is sent back to the country she came from.*

Discrimination

Since that time, Hispanic people have discovered that being successful in the United States is hard. Speaking Spanish instead of English has made things harder for them. If you don't speak English, it's hard to vote. If you don't speak English, it's hard to learn in school. It's hard to get a job if you don't know English.

This child deserves the rights and privileges every other American enjoys.

Latinos celebrate their identity.

Some Hispanic immigrants want to live close to other people who have the same culture and language. They move into neighborhoods where almost everyone speaks Spanish. Stores sell Latin American food. The neighborhoods are called *barrios*. When you're in a new country, it helps to have other people around who understand you.

But it might also make it hard for other people to accept you. That's what is happening in the United States. Some Americans think that Hispanics should speak English. They don't like the barrios. They say that if Hispanics want to live in the United States, they should become just like other Americans. They should speak English. They should act like other Americans.

But think about it. If you moved to another country, wouldn't it be hard to stop doing things you were used to doing? You would still want to eat the same food. You'd want to speak your own language. You'd want to celebrate the same holidays you'd always had. It's the same for Hispanic immigrants. They're proud of their culture. It helps make them strong. It makes them special. And it can make the United States stronger, too.

But sometimes other Americans are scared of the differences they see in Hispanic Americans. They think that Hispanics are too different. Sometimes, people think Hispanics aren't as good as other Americans. Then they treat them differently. That's called discrimination.

The Battle for Civil Rights

The Hispanic American battle for civil rights has not been easy. And it's not over. Millions of immigrants are now U.S. citizens, but they still suffer from discrimination. Low wages, poor housing, and bad education are normal for lots of Hispanic Americans.

Hispanics have made gains in civil rights, however. The fight for civil rights was strongest at the end of the 1960s and the beginning of the 1970s. Like black Americans, other groups had to fight for their rights. This was the time when women started fighting for their rights. So did homosexuals. And so do Hispanic Americans.

But not many people know about the Hispanic fight for civil rights. TV, radio, and newspapers didn't tell Americans about what was going on. Since not many people knew what was happening, not many people could support the fight. People on the East Coast of the United States didn't even know what was going on with Hispanics in the Southwest.

The people who did care about the fight mostly spoke Spanish. Leaders made speeches in Spanish. English-speaking Americans couldn't understand what was going on. But Hispanic leaders worked hard to change things.

César Chávez worked with many people to bring rights to farm workers.

LATINO AMERICAN CIVIL RIGHTS

César Chávez

César Chávez was a Mexican American farm worker. He had had a hard life growing up. His family was poor. They lived in dirty, crowded houses. His teachers didn't care if he learned or not. César knew that farm workers weren't treated well. They didn't make enough money to live well.

In the 1960s and '70s, César led the fight for Hispanic rights. He wanted the owners of big farms to treat their Hispanic workers fairly. He started the United Farm Workers Union. It fought to protect the rights of thousands of workers on farms across the country. The Union is still strong in the United States today, fifty years later.

César Chávez

César led a strike, which means that workers refused to work. They agreed to go back to work only if they got fair pay. The strike almost shut down many farms. The strikers stayed strong. They won their battle.

César made people notice Hispanic farm workers. For the first time, many people thought about Hispanic rights.

Reies López Tijerina

Reies López Tijerina was another leader in the Hispanic civil rights movement of the 1960s and '70s. He wanted to give land back to Hispanic families who had lost their land back in the 1800s. He wasn't afraid to break the law to stand up for what he believed. He ended up in prison.

Dolores Huerta worked with César Chávez for farm workers' civil rights. Since then, she has continued to work for people's rights.

LATINO AMERICAN CIVIL RIGHTS

Dolores Huerta

Dolores Huerta was an important part of the United Farm Workers Union strike. Many years later, she was in a peaceful **protest** against the **policies** of George H. W. Bush. The police didn't want her to protest. Dolores ended up getting hurt. She fought back in the courts—and she won. Her fight changed how the police deal with protests. Now fewer people get hurt.

Justice!

These people are leaders in the fight for Hispanic civil rights. But many people have been part of the fight for justice. This means they make sure that people are treated fairly. This fight doesn't only help Hispanic Americans. It helps us all. It makes the world a safer, better place for everyone to live.

A **protest** *is when people gather together to show they disagree with something or want something changed.*

Policies *are the basic rules a government uses to make decisions.*

chapter 3
Hispanic Civil Rights at Work

Imagine working in a huge field, picking strawberries all day long. The sun beats down on your back. You aren't given any water. There's no shade. After your long day at work, you go back to your trailer. You share the trailer with ten other people. There's no toilet. You have to sleep on the floor. To top it all off, you don't even make as much money as many teenagers make babysitting or mowing lawns! But you work so hard because you want to send money back to your family in Mexico. You know they have even less money.

Millions of Hispanic people live like this every day. Many of them travel around from place to place, following jobs. Maybe they pick grapes in one state for a month. When that's done, they move fifty miles to pick watermelons in another state. We call them migrant workers. Most of them work in fields, picking fruits and vegetables. Some work in factories.

The Hispanic civil rights movement had a lot to do with migrant workers. César Chávez worked for a long time to make migrant workers' lives better. He helped them have a say in how they were treated. He signed up Hispanic citizens to vote in elections.

Laws Aren't Always Enough

Over the years, the United States has passed laws that protect migrant workers. Some people don't think they do enough. Many employers who hire migrant workers don't even follow the laws. Migrant workers are still treated badly.

Migrant workers don't have much power. They don't want to lose their jobs. They don't want to be sent back to Mexico. So they're afraid to complain. Instead of complaining, they accept low pay. They work and live in bad situations.

Our laws haven't gotten rid of discrimination. European Americans can send their children to good schools. They live in safe neighborhoods. They can afford to go to the doctor. They can pay for college. They grow up in homes without drugs or violence. If you get a good education, you can get a job more easily when you grow up. So a lot of European Americans have jobs that pay a lot of money. They can be lawyers, scientists, or professors.

The Hispanic presence adds color throughout the Southwest.

Migrant workers' children stand beneath the sign for the government's Farm Security Administration in the 1940s.

S. DEPARTMENT
AGRICULTURE
RM SECURITY ADMINISTRATION
m Workers Community

29

On the other hand, many **minorities** can't get good jobs. They live in dangerous neighborhoods. They don't have enough money for good food. They can't afford to go to the doctor when they're sick. They can't send their kids to good schools, or pay for college. They end up with jobs that pay less.

This isn't ALWAYS true of course! Some European American families can't afford college. Sometimes white Americans live in dangerous neighborhoods. And some minorities have good jobs. Many Hispanic and black Americans go to college. But more white Americans can afford school, doctors, and good food. Fewer minorities can.

Even if a minority is qualified for a job, he or she still might not get it. Some employers would rather hire a white person. This is discrimination. It's against the law.

Migrant workers protesting for better conditions in the 1950s.

The Law

Americans have discriminated against minorities for a long time. But we also have lots of laws to tackle discrimination.

LATINO AMERICAN CIVIL RIGHTS

The same Latina woman who received a Bronze Medal after her son was killed in the Korean War also faced discrimination from other Americans.

The first big step came in 1954. The Supreme Court made an important decision in a case called *Brown versus the Board of Education*. The decision got rid of legal **segregation**. Before, white people and black people or Hispanic people had to use different bathrooms. They had to travel on different train cars. There wasn't any good reason. It was just that white people thought minorities were not as good as them. They didn't want to share schools or even bathrooms with them. After the court decision, everyone used the same space. Americans were one step closer to **equality** for all people.

Starting in the 1960s, laws were passed that protected minorities in the workplace. Other laws helped minorities get good jobs and get into college.

> **Segregation** *is when a minority group is unfairly kept out of certain places, like schools or restaurants.*
>
> **Equality** *is when everyone is treated the same way.*

Some Americans didn't like what the government was doing. They were afraid of the new laws. They didn't want to change how things were. But usually, people accepted the new laws.

During the 1960s, most people in the United States were doing well. There were enough jobs to go around. In fact, sometimes employers had a hard time finding all the workers they needed. Employers understood they needed to hire minorities to keep their businesses growing.

That changed in the 1970s. Now there weren't as many jobs anymore. Employers didn't need minorities to work for them. White Americans who didn't have jobs felt jealous of minorities who did have jobs. They were especially jealous of Hispanics and black Americans. The country's leaders started to change the laws.

A civil rights protest in the 1960s.

Hispanics in the 1980s and Beyond

In the 1980s, Hispanics continued to deal with discrimination at work. They earned much less money each year than white Americans. They stayed in low-level jobs instead of moving up to higher-paid jobs.

Let's say a white American and a Hispanic American were both hired to work as waiters in a restaurant. They were both just as good at their jobs. But the Hispanic person is on time more often. He doesn't ever mess up an order. The boss is still more likely to make the white person the head waiter. The Hispanic waiter won't get a better job—just because he's Hispanic.

That sounds unfair, doesn't it? It is! Discrimination is very unfair. It still happens today. We still have a long way to go to get rid of discrimination in the workplace.

This girl deserves equal treatment as all other citizens of the United States.

chapter 4
Hispanic Civil Rights in the Home

In the United States, having a safe, clean home is a basic human right. It could be a house or an apartment. All people have the right to a home. Without a home, what would we do when it rains? Where would we sleep? How would we cook our food? Having a home helps people survive. It makes them happy.

Early Discrimination

Lots of people came to the United States to find a home. There was lots of land and space during America's early years. There weren't that many people. But over the years, the number of people in the United States grew. More people took up more space.

When the United States was young, it only took up the eastern part of North America. Americans knew about the wide-open western part of the continent. They wanted to move there, where there was more land. Native people lived there, but there was still a lot of empty land. White settlers moved west in wagons.

Even when the settlers found other people on the land, they didn't care. They made the Native people leave. They pushed out Hispanics who already called the West home. Nothing stopped the settlers. Not even the law.

Now many Hispanic Americans lived on land owned by other people. They had to farm the land for other people. Families often barely earned enough money to feed themselves.

Since those early times when settlers forced Hispanics off their land, it's gotten worse. To feel safer and to help each other, some Hispanics lived in communities called *barrios*. Everyone spoke Spanish. Barrios let Hispanics keep their language and other traditions. They also made

An assembly at a Latino school in the 1940s.

LATINO AMERICAN CIVIL RIGHTS

In the 1960s, blacks and Latinos spoke out against segregated schools. They wanted their children to have the same chances to learn that white children had.

37

The immigration building in Miami, Florida. Many Hispanic Americans are recent immigrants to the United States.

other Americans angry. Some people thought that Hispanics should live with everyone else.

Housing Discrimination Today

Barrios still exist today. Even if Hispanics don't want to live in barrios, it's hard for them to live somewhere else.

Today, U.S. law says that all families have the right to own a home. It doesn't matter what their race or religion is. But not everyone obeys these laws. Hispanic families still have trouble buying homes.

In 1968, the United States signed a law called the Civil Rights Act. It said that all Americans must have basic civil rights. Buying or renting a home was one of these rights. Under the law, everyone had the chance to buy or rent a home. They could be Hispanic, Asian, or any other minority. **Landlords** couldn't make minori-

Landlords *are people who own the houses and apartments other people pay to live in.*

LATINO AMERICAN CIVIL RIGHTS

ties pay higher rent. Banks couldn't make it harder for minorities to get loans to buy houses.

The Civil Rights Act is a good first step, but minorities still face discrimination when trying to find a home. It's still harder for minorities to get a safe home than it is for white Americans.

Hispanic Americans have the hardest time of anyone. This is partly because some landlords, banks, and home sellers ignore the law. They don't want to sell homes to Hispanic American. They charge them more money. Sometimes they refuse to show them houses in neighborhoods that aren't Hispanic.

Justice means that all people can live in safe, comfortable homes. Everyone has the right to a home!

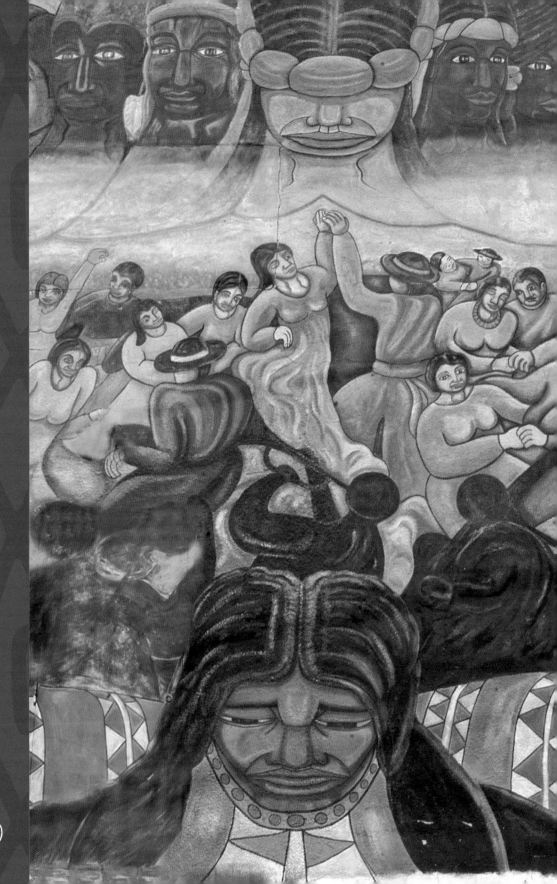

chapter 5
Hispanic Civil Rights and Politics

Politics is the way the government works. It's how laws get made. Politics influences your life every day. You go to school because the law says all kids have to. Your favorite state park is open because laws created it. You wear your seat belt because of the law.

Politics is also important for civil rights. Making things fair for all Americans can only happen through laws. Minorities like Hispanics need people to represent them in politics.

Hispanic Power

Right now, almost 50 million Hispanic Americans live in the United States. More move here or are born here every day. **Politicians** have noticed that there are lots of Hispanics. Politicians need lots of people to vote for them if they want to win elections. Many politicians now spend a lot of time and money trying to make Hispanics happy. They want Hispanic Americans to vote for them. They want those 50 million votes!

But there are very few politicians who are Hispanic. There are lots of Hispanic Americans, but not very many Hispanic American representatives, governors, or mayors. There has never been a Hispanic president. Even though the United States has so many Hispanics, the government doesn't. Hispanic Americans need more people in the government who really understand their problems.

> **Politicians** *are people who work in the government and make the rules other people have to follow.*

Hispanic Americans also need more voters to stand up for them. One problem is that not all Hispanics vote. That's true of all Americans, Hispanic or not. Only a small percentage of Americans vote on election day. The number of Hispanic Americans who vote is especially small. There are lots of reasons for this. A big reason is poverty. Poor people may not be able to read about elections as well. They often don't trust politicians as much. Sometimes they can't get

A 1960s protest march in New York City for equal rights.

LATINO AMERICAN CIVIL RIGHTS

The face of the future.

to the places where they would vote because they don't have cars or they can't take the bus. Many Hispanics are poor, so fewer of them vote.

Another problem is the word "Hispanic." Not all people that the United States calls Hispanic FEEL Hispanic. Just because someone calls you by a name, doesn't mean you think it fits you!

The term Hispanic American actually refers to people who come from twenty-two different countries. There are even different cultures within each one of those countries. Not all Hispanics share a religion. There are Catholics, Protestants, Jews, Buddhists, and others. There are lots of other differences between different Hispanics.

Because Hispanics feel different from each other, it's harder to join together. Mexican Americans might find it hard to support a Cuban American politician. Or a person who just came to the United

Children like this will grow
up speaking two languages.

States might not agree with a Hispanic leader whose family has been in the United States for 100 years.

Unity

Other things bring Hispanics together. Sometimes different Hispanic groups unite and fight for one goal. Most Hispanics support laws that help families and make education better. They sometimes support **bilingual** education. Bilingual education offers classes in both English and Spanish. Many Hispanics hope that bilingual education will help their children do well in school.

Most Hispanic Americans are also interested in **immigration laws**. A lot of immigration to the United States is from Latin American countries. Any laws that the United States makes about immigration will affect all these countries. Hispanics might not always agree about how the United States should deal with immigration. They do agree that it's an important problem!

A new issue that Hispanic Americans care about is the English-only movement in the United States. Some people want to make English America's official language. The government would only use English. This would mean that people who only speak Spanish would find voting very hard. It would be hard for them to pay taxes. Applying for jobs or even going to the hospital would be hard, too. Bilingual education wouldn't be an option. It isn't a national law yet, but some states are English-only.

These are big problems Hispanic Americans face. They will only be able to deal with these issues if they work together.

Bilingual *means that something is done in two languages.*

Immigration laws *are the rules about who can move from one country to another and how a person can become a citizen of her new country.*

chapter 6
Hispanic Civil Rights and Education

Going to school might seem like a chore. Or maybe you really love school. Either way, education is really important. You learn about the world. You learn about other people. And you learn skills you can use in a job later on. People who don't finish high school are more likely to be out of work.

Most jobs in the United States require thinking. You learn how to think in school. If you don't go to a good school where you learn how to think, you don't get to practice thinking. We all know that practice makes perfect. So if you don't practice thinking, it will be hard for you to get a job where you need that skill. Owning businesses, going to college, and getting well-paying jobs are a lot harder if you don't learn how to think in school.

How Does Hispanic Education Measure Up?

Hispanic Americans get almost the worst education of any group of people in America. Lots of Hispanics don't have a high school diploma. As a result, only a few Hispanics have high-paying jobs like doctor, lawyer, or company manager.

Education starts early. Getting an education even before kindergarten actually helps you succeed later. Hispanics are less likely to send their children to preschool programs.

In elementary school, Hispanic American children are less likely to be in gifted programs than white American students. Hispanic children are often held behind a grade. They also drop out more often.

But it's not because they're stupid! Hispanic Americans are just as smart as anyone else. But they often have to go to schools that don't give them a good education. Their schools don't have enough money. There aren't enough teachers to give every student enough attention.

Drug use is often a problem. There aren't enough computers or textbooks to go around. These things keep them from getting a good education.

Recent immigrants in Miami wait for assistance at Church World Service, an agency that provides job training, English classes, and other services.

Some Hispanic American students don't speak English. It's hard to take tests if you don't speak the language! It's hard to read textbooks and write essays if you can't use the language you know. You can be really smart, but if you can't read or write English, you can't do well at school. Some states, like California, only let schools teach in English. This means it's really hard to do well at school if you only know Spanish.

These problems in elementary and high schools mean fewer Hispanics go to college, too. Even students who finish high school might not go

LATINO AMERICAN CIVIL RIGHTS

The Youth Co-op in Miami assists Hispanic immigrants.

49

Latinos at a street celebration.

to college. Only one-third of Hispanic Americans go to college. That's a lot less than white Americans. The students who do go to college often need extra help. Their grades are often lower than the grades of people from other groups.

Segregation in School

It's illegal to send minority students to different schools. That's called segregation. However, segregation in schools still happens anyway.

White American families often have enough money to live in suburbs and send their kids to good schools. Minority families usually have to live in poorer neighborhoods. They have to send their kids to schools that aren't very good. Some schools are made up almost entirely of minority students. In places where lots of Hispanics live, some schools are mostly Hispanic.

LATINO AMERICAN CIVIL RIGHTS

Still, that's different from the kind of segregation that used to be legal. During the early 1900s, schools were separated into white schools, black schools, and Hispanic schools. In the Southwest, Hispanics were sent to special schools separate from everyone else. They were not as good as the white schools. Hispanics and blacks fought back. Since then, the United States has made all segregation illegal.

But we also need to make sure Hispanics don't get stuck in schools that don't teach them what they need to learn!

Hope for the Future

Hispanic Americans know this. They want programs that improve education for all students, from kindergarten to college. They often support preschool programs. They want gifted programs. They also support programs that get students into college.

A counselor provides education advice at a Latino agency.

Miami, Florida, has many Latino communities.

There are some colleges that teach mostly Hispanic students. They get money from the government to help these students. It might not be the best situation, since Hispanic students are separated from others. But if the only other option is not going to college at all, then it definitely helps.

It's still hard for Hispanics to go to college. College costs a lot of money. Schools are also getting more expensive every year. Poor students, including Hispanics, can't afford to pay even more. Some students work one, two, or even three jobs while still taking classes! No wonder they can't get good grades.

It's also hard for many Hispanic students to get into top colleges. Schools like to take people who have the highest grades in high school. They want students with the highest test scores. Lots of Hispanics haven't gone to very good schools. They don't have very good grades or test scores. Then they don't get into college.

Bilingual education is a big debate. Should Spanish be used in schools? Some people say yes, others say no. In fact, some Hispanics actually think that it shouldn't. They want their kids to speak English.

Right now, the government spends lots of money on bilingual education. In the future, politicians could decide to stop spending that money. Or people could vote to end bilingual programs. Only the future will tell what will happen.

The number of Hispanics in the United States is growing. They are already the biggest minority group in the country. Things are changing in the United States. You can hear Spanish in many big cities, and sometimes in smaller towns. The United States has a Hispanic Heritage Month from September 15 to October 15. Lots of cities have Puerto Rican, Cuban, or Mexican festivals that celebrate Hispanics. Americans enjoy celebrating Hispanic holidays. They love eating tacos and salsa. Hispanic Americans are changing the country.

Fewer Hispanic Americans are immigrants these days. More and more are born in the United States. They have never lived anywhere else. More

If Latino citizens exercise their privilege to vote, they could become a powerful political force.

Hispanic citizens means that Hispanics will have more say in how we run the country.

America is a nation of immigrants. We come from many different places. Together, we work to make our country strong. We need each other.

The United States needs Hispanic Americans, just like it needs all its people. Hispanic Americans do important jobs. They bring their beautiful cultures to America. They share their delicious foods. They help make the United States strong and special.

LATINOS TODAY

In the twenty-first century, Latinos have become the largest minority group in the United States. (A minority is a group of people different from most of the other people in the country. Blacks, Asians, and Latinos are all minorities in the United States—but in a country like Kenya in Africa, for example, whites would be a minority.) In 2010, there were almost 50 million Hispanics (Latinos) in the United States. That's about 15 percent of America's total population— which means that if you had 100 Americans in a room, 15 of them would be likely to be Hispanics. Most Latinos,

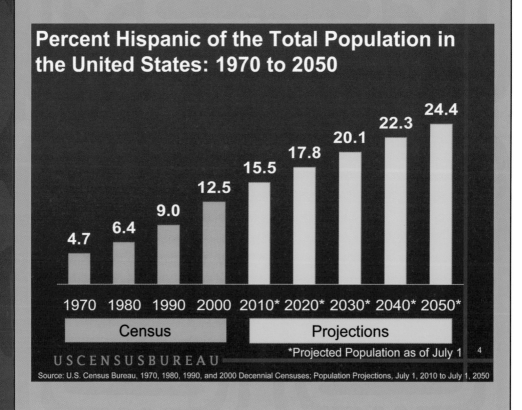

Percent Hispanic of the Total Population in the United States: 1970 to 2050

1970	1980	1990	2000	2010*	2020*	2030*	2040*	2050*
4.7	6.4	9.0	12.5	15.5	17.8	20.1	22.3	24.4

Census | Projections

*Projected Population as of July 1 [4]

U S C E N S U S B U R E A U

Source: U.S. Census Bureau, 1970, 1980, 1990, and 2000 Decennial Censuses; Population Projections, July 1, 2010 to July 1, 2050

Hispanic Origin by Type: 2006

Type of origin	Number	Percent
Total	44,252,278	100.0
Mexican	28,339,354	64.0
Puerto Rican	3,987,947	9.0
Cuban	1,520,276	3.4
Dominican	1,217,225	2.8
Central American	3,372,090	7.6
South American	2,421,297	5.5
Other Hispanic	3,394,089	7.7

USCENSUSBUREAU

Source: U.S. Census Bureau, 2006 American Community Survey

however, live in the western part of the United States, although more and more of them are moving to the East as well.

These Americans have roots in both Spain and the Americas. They have taken what's best from their past. They've added that to all the good things in the United States. They have faced a lot hardship along the way. They have had to fight for their rights. They are still fighting those battles. But Latinos today are becoming successful. They are doing a good job in every area of American life!

Time Line

1100   Mayan Civilization is at its strongest in Central America.

1325   Aztecs conquer Mexico.

1438   Inca rule begins in Peru.

1492   Christopher Columbus lands on the island of Hispaniola (Santo Domingo and Haiti).

1503   Hernan Cortes arrives in Hispaniola.

1521   Cortes defeats the Aztecs in Mexico.

1532   Francisco Pizarro conquers the Inca in Peru.

1610   Santa Fe, New Mexico, is built.

1690   First Spanish settlement in Texas is built.

1769   Franciscan missionary Junipero Serra builds the first mission in California. He will eventually build ten missions up and down California.

1817   Simón Bolivar begins his fight for independence from Spain in Colombia, Venezuela, and Ecuador.

1821   Mexico declares independence from Spain.

1845   Texas becomes part of the United States.

1846   Mexican-American War begins. New Mexico (which includes modern-day New Mexico, Arizona, southern Colorado, southern Utah, and southern Utah) becomes part of the United States.

1868 The Fourteenth Amendment to the U.S. Constitution says that all Hispanics born in the United States are U.S. citizens.

1898 Puerto Rico and Cuba become part of the United States.

1901 Cuba becomes an independent country.

1902 The Reclamation Act is passed, take away land from many Hispanic Americans.

1910 The beginning of the Mexican Revolution sends thousands of Mexicans north to settle in the American Southwest.

1943 U.S. government allows Mexican farmworkers to enter the United States.

1959 Fidel Castro takes over Cuba. Many Cubans immigrate to the United States.

1970s Violence in Central America spurs massive migration to the United States.

1990 President George Bush appoints the first woman and first Hispanic surgeon general of the United States: Antonia C. Novello.

2003 Hispanics are pronounced the nation's largest minority group surpassing African Americans—after new Census figures are released showing the U.S. Hispanic population at 37.1 million as of July 2001.

2006 According to the Census Bureau, the number of Hispanic-owned businesses grew three times faster than the national average for all U.S. businesses.

Find Out More

IN BOOKS

Berry, Joy. *Mine & Yours: Human Rights for Kids.* New York, N.Y.: Amnesty International Publications, 2005.

Cohn, Diana and Francisco Delgado. *Si Se Puede/Yes We Can: Janitor Strike in L.A.* El Paso, Tex.: Cinco Puntos, 2005

Krull, Kathleen. *Harvesting Hope: The Story of Cesar Chavez.* San Diego, Calif.: Harcourt, Inc., 2003.

Petrillo, Valerie. *A Kid's Guide to Latino History*. Chicago, Ill.: Chicago Review Press, Inc., 2009.

Taylor-Butler, Christine. *The Bill of Rights*. New York, N.Y.: Scholastic, Inc., 2008.

Truck, Mary. *The Civil Rights Movement for Kids.* Chicago, Ill.: Chicago Review Press, Inc., 2000.

ON THE INTERNET

Bill of Rights
www.historyforkids.org/learn/northamerica/after1500/government/
  billofrights.htm

Cesar Chavez
www.myhero.com/go/hero.asp?hero=c_chavez

Delores Huerta
www.lasculturas.com/aa/bio/bioDoloresHuerta.htm

Hispanic Heritage
www.pbskids.org/mayaandmiguel/english/stunts/hhm/index.html

Hispanic Rights Activists
www.lasculturas.com/aa/bio/bioActivist.php

History of the Civil Rights Movement
www.pbskids.org/wayback/civilrights

Latino Civil Rights History
www.tolerance.org/activity/latino-civil-rights-timeline-1903-2006

National Council of La Raza (Hispanic Rights Organization)
www.nclr.org

United Farm Workers
www.ufw.org

Index

Picture Credits

Benjamin Stewart: p. 19, 28, 38, 43, 48, 49, 51, 52

Carin Zissis, carinzissis@hotmail.com: p. 44

Bouch, Michelle: p. 23

Charles A. Hack: 18, 20. 50

Eric Guo: p. 24

The Justo A. Martí Photographic Collection, Centro de Estudios Puertorriqueños, Hunter College, CUNY, Photographer unknown: p. 31

Library of Congress: p. 29

The National Archives and Records Administration: p. 32, 37

PhotoDisc: p. 54

Photos.com: p. 33

The Records of the Offices of the Government of Puerto Rico in the U.S., Centro de Estudios Puertorriqueños, Hunter College, CUNY, Photographer unknown: p. 17, 30, 42

The Ruth M. Reynolds Papers, Centro de Estudios Puertorriqueños, Hunter College, CUNY, Photographer unknown: p. 10. 36

Santiago Iglesias, Centro de Estudios Puertorriqueños, Hunter College, CUNY, Photographer unknown: p. 22

About the Author and the Consultant

Thomas Arkham has studied history for most of his life. He is an editor, author, and avid collector who lives in Upstate New York.

Dr. José E. Limón is professor of Mexican-American Studies at the University of Texas at Austin where he has taught for twenty-five years. He has authored over forty articles and three books on Latino cultural studies and history. He lectures widely to academic audiences, civic groups, and K–12 educators.